THE OMER
AND THE KABBALAH

Forty-Nine Blessings Leading
to the Giving of the Torah

MAX AMICHAI HEPPNER

THE OMER AND THE KABBALAH
Forty-Nine Blessings Leading to the Giving of the Torah
by Max Amichai Heppner

The Omer counts that most influenced this book were those beginning
March 31, 2018, April 9, 2009, and April 20, 2000

Published by:

Heppner Books

www.heppnerbooks.com

Copyright © 2018 Max Amichai Heppner

ISBN: 978-1-7348953-0-8

Cover illustration: Classical oil painting by Rembrandt van Rijn:
Moses Presenting the Tablets of the Law, signaling the end of the Omer Count

Contents

Torah's Imperative for Counting the Omer

(Lev. 23:15-16)

You shall count seven full weeks from . . [the eve of the second day of Passover], the day you brought the sheaf (Omer) of the wave offering. You shall count fifty days to the day of the the seventh Sabbath. Then you shall present a grain offering of new grain [wheat] to the Lord.

Preface

Counting the Omer.

The *Omer* [rhymes with Homer] fills the time period between *Pesach* (Pay-sach) "Passover" and *Shavuot* (Shav-voo-oat), the Feast of Weeks. Practitioners schedule the Omer count somewhere between sundown and midnight. Both the requirement of the count and the time period in which the counting should occur are based on Torah verses. [Respectively, Lev. 23: 15-16; and Gen. 1: 4].

The count starts with a blessing followed by the exact count that was reached that day:

בָּרוּךְ אַתָּה יְיָ אֱלֹהֵינוּ מֶלֶךְ הָעוֹלָם, אֲשֶׁר קִדְּשָׁנוּ
בְּמִצְוֹתָיו, וְצִוָּנוּ עַל סְפִירַת הָעוֹמֶר:

הַיּוֹם יוֹם אֶחָד לָעוֹמֶר:

Baruch ata adonay, Eloheynu Melech ha-Olam,
asher kid'shanu bemitzvotav vetzivanu al sefirat ha-Omer.
Ha-yom, yom echad l'Omer
(Blessed are You, God and King of All, who makes us holy by directing us on the path by counting the days of the Omer. Today is the 1st day of the Omer.)

In taking up this practice, Kabbalists made the count a spiritual experience, and that's the intent of this book. Since I started this practice, I have new insights in these daily blessings—most of which bring me new light and joy. Some can be sad and heavy, like what I discovered this year by digging deeper into Hod (week 4). I learned the deep truth in my father's favorite saying, "Anything done to extremes is no good." Even in the case of *splendor*, I saw that looking good carried to extremes isn't really good at all.

At first, people wanting to add spirituality to the Omer count drew on various Biblical, Talmudic, or other erudite passages. (A favorite was Psalm 67 because the Hebrew text, which contains 49 words, matches the number of days in the Omer.) Later, Kabbalists composed blessings specific to each Omer day, like we're doing here.

Meditators say, in general, that it takes about 40 days to complete a spiritual journey. Torah agrees! Scripture tells us that Moses meditated in communion with God on Mt. Sinai for 40 days before receiving the Tablets of the Law.

3

By extending our spiritual practice to 49 days, we can go even deeper. Even the number of days in the Omer count are spiritually super-lucky. Seven days in seven weeks give us the square of seven, a number which, standing alone, already is considered lucky.

For an entire 49 days plus the holy day of Shavuot, we're lit up by light reflected from Passover, arguably the most widely celebrated Jewish holiday. Passover streams spiritual light into the Jewish universe like a solar flare, and people who revel in it don't want to let go of it.

In Temple times, Pilgrims arriving in Jerusalem for Passover tended to remain in town for the entire Omer. For the extra 49 days, they had a joyful time tenting around the Temple Mount, happy not to travel all the way home after Passover and then head back again to Jerusalem in time for Shavuot.

Even when Shavuot was over, they continued celebrating, naming the day of their departure *Isru Chag*, an observance to bundle the joy of Passover, Omer, and Shavuot and make it last for the rest of the year. They said their celebration realizes Verse 27 of Psalm 118, which says, "Bind (*Isru*) the festival offering with cords to the corners of the altar."

As early Jewish followers of Jesus (the proto-orthodox Christians) developed their own observance, they added the Day of Shavuot to the Omer count. That increased the number of Omer days to 50, and they renamed it *Pentecost (from* the Greek *pentēkostē hēmera,* fiftieth day). Scholars such as John Oakes hold that public Christianity began on the day of Pentecost [See Acts: 2.] Events described there are the first recorded example of salvation in the name of Jesus Christ being preached to the general public. [See: "evidenceforChristianity.org/when-did-christianity-begin-r/]

Christian observers added to the import of the Pentecost by noting that all of the post-Crucifixion appearances of Jesus noted in the Gospels occur during the Omer. For example, on the first day of the Omer, Jesus appears to Mary Magdalene and then to Simon Peter (Mark 16:9). These appearances continue until the 50th day, when Jesus said: "Do not let your hearts be troubled. You [who] believe in God, believe also in me. My Father's house has many rooms; if that were not so, would I have told you that I am going there to prepare a place for you?"

All of us should feel included in this beautiful blessing!

Pesach: The Launching Pad.

Pesach (the Passover) started as a springtime agricultural festival. While we were principally herdsmen, we celebrated the arrival of the new lambs in the sheep flocks. When we turned our attention to farming, part of the emphasis shifted to the ripening of the first grain harvest: Barley.

Still, sheep remained the major sacrificial totem of spring, and the Pascal sacrifice stayed a symbol of thanks to God for good harvests.

As the Jewish religion developed, sheep (and in particular the lambs) became more symbolic of Jewish culture. While neighboring peoples had cattle as their totem, we symbolized our new life view by sheep. Violating the sheep totem made the apostasy of Aaron [Ex. 32] all the more extreme. Not only were the rebels to whom he toadied denying the primacy of God and the leadership of Moses, but they also defied the newly-found totem of Israel. A golden lamb would not have been as defiant as the Golden Calf.

Lambs are at the heart of the story of our emergence as a free people. God freed us from slavery in Egypt by having us paint lamb's blood on the outside door posts of our houses. This was the signal for the Angel of Death implementing the Tenth Plague to "pass over" the houses of the Jews [Ex. 12:11], leading to the name of **Passover.**

To the early Christian Jews, of course, Jesus the Savior, became the sacrificial lamb,"who takes away the sin of the world" [John 1:29].

The Omer: The Vehicle of Travel.

The Omer has us travel step by step, day by day, from Passover to Shavuot, and the Kabbalists felt a spiritual loss if they missed the midnight deadline the rabbis set for this daily practice. Torah tells us to begin the count on the eve of the Second Day of *Pesach*, the day ". . . on which you bring the sheaf of wave offering [of barley to the Temple as a sacrifice]." [Lev. 23:15-16]. The amount of barley threshed from the wave offering must be at least an *Omer* (two dry quarts), thereby lending its name to the *Omer* count.

Barley ripens earlier than wheat, which economically is a more important crop. After the barley offering, people watched nervously as their wheat was growing, with a prayer each day that the wheat should grow and yield well. Each *week* in the process was honored, leading to the very name of the holiday of *Shevuot*—literally "weeks."

Sefirot: The Energy for Travel.

Kabbalists assigned each week of the Omer a quality called a *Sefirah* (pronounced Seff-ee-raw), the plural of which is *Sefirot* (pronounced Seff-ee-roat, with a meaning related to the English "spheres.") In modern physiology, the *Sefirot* have been identified as "energy centers" or "nerve ganglia" located in specific areas of the human body. *Sefirot* also find a parallel in the "Chakras" of the Hindu-Sanskrit spiritual lexicon.

A basic tenet in Kabbalah holds that the *Sefirot* make up the *Etz Chayim* (Aits Chay-yim), the "Tree of Life." This imaginary tree represents the structure of your spiritual self as well as the structure by which God holds the Universe together. During the Omer count, the Tree of Life invites you to open up each of its *Sefirot* in the sense of "opening your heart." This expression is right on target because your heart is right at the center of the seven *Sefirot* of the Omer count. If you can open up your heart, you can open up your other *Sefirot* as well.

Going a step further than associating a Sefirah with each Omer week, the kabbalists also imbued every *day* of each week with its own Sefirah; the combination enriches the blessing for each day by enabling the user to visualize how the week's Sefirah is influenced when the day's "small" Sefirah is inserted into it. It is a bit like seeing how the coffee in a large mug changes in color by just adding some cream.

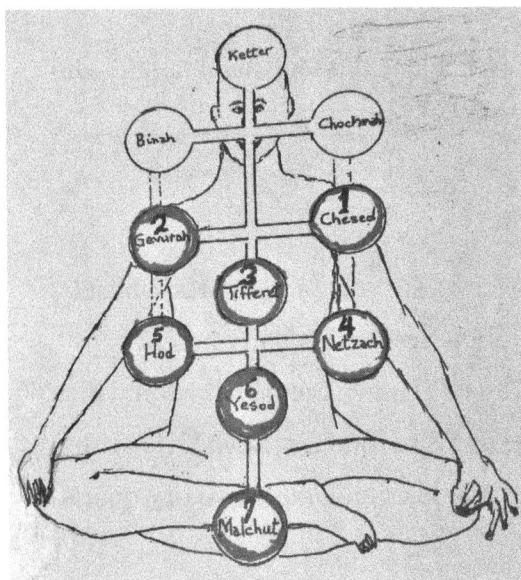

My schematic drawing of the spiritual Tree of Life imposed on a human body shows that while the traditional tree has ten Sefirot, the Omer count uses only the seven lower ones. I heard a Kabbalist explain that the upper three "are too etherial for a mundane counting of days."

In the following pages, I will share with you how each day's configuration of Sefirot (the week's combined with the day's Sefirah) has inspired me. Rabbi Barry Silver of Congregation L'Dor Va-Dor in Boca Raton, Florida, says that experiencing this type of inspiration lets us "open our heart and mind to the awe, wonder, and rapturous appreciation of the symmetry, majesty, and miracles which abound in the natural world and within each of us." [Florida Jewish Journal, May 16, 2018, page 16.]

Fortunately for the Jews of today, most of whom are not wheat farmers, the Kabbalists made the seven weeks of counting into a devotional practice. Their instructions lead us day by day, step by step, from the yoke of slavery toward the joy of freedom—from *Pesach* to *Shevuot*. The visual imagery of *Pesach* is the dramatic, dry-land ford across the Sea of Reeds. The equally dramatic transmittal of the Tablets of the Law at Sinai is the visual imagery for Shavuot. (See the famous representation of this scene in Rembrandt's painting reproduced on the cover.

—Max Amichai Heppner

FIRST WEEK: CHESED

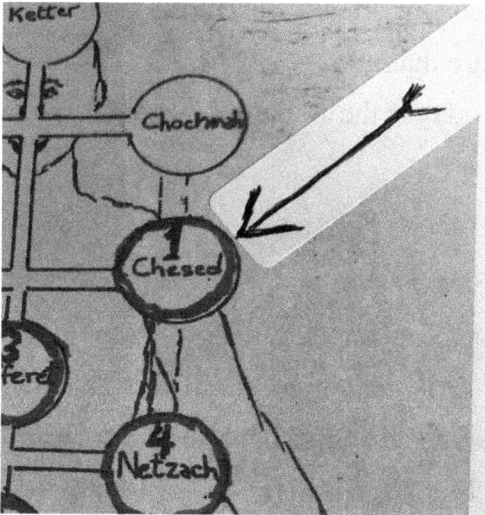

Chesed (Chess-ed) is a poetic concept in Hebrew that seriously challenges the translator. The universe of meaning in *Chesed* contains not only *grace*, but also love, kindness, mercy, righteousness, and charity. It is *Chesed* to which the beggar appeals and *Chesed* that inspires the *Chasidim* "Righteous Observant Ones" to appeal to God for merciful acceptance. The Kabbalists call *Chesed* both "The Right Hand of Mercy" and "The Left Hand of Creation" (or vice-versa, because in the Mirror of Life, everything is easily reversed).

The Grace in *Chesed* is the Pure Soul that God has invested in all human beings. We merit our pure soul through the blessing of *Chesed,* so that we don't have to earn our right to exist. When a Jewish philosopher paraphrases Descartes, he says: "I received *Chesed,* therefore I am." And he adds: "The universe is founded on *Chesed."*

Chesed is associated with truth—with uttering pure speech. God spoke in *Chesed* and created the Universe. God keeps speaking in *Chesed* to keep the Universe moving and intact. Similarly, *Chesed* requires us to govern our speech, which is seen as our own creative power.

Jewish sages teach: "Be your word! Your life gains in validity as your word gains in truthfulness."

First blessing: Inner Grace

Chesed sh'b'Chesed (Chess-ed shah bah Chess-ed) "Righteousness within Righteousness" is the spark that launches the First Creation, the Essence of Creation, the kernel of truth, and the actualization of mercy.

This first day of the Omer is extra-special; it is the starting gate of our spiritual and joyful Omer journey. The inspiration of this day helps us recreate the image of crossing difficult waters on dry land into a future of freedom; and then marching confidently behind Moses, our spiritual guide, toward an investiture with Torah.

Our people, pictured in the Biblical story of Exodus as persistent grumblers and groaners, didn't mutter a word of complaint that first day—streaming exultantly out of Egypt, the Narrow Place, the House of Bondage into the Opportunity of Freedom.

This Sefirah stimulates us to laugh, dance, shout, and celebrate. We jubilate "Hallelujah. We're free at last." We rejoice that Pharaoh, the Hard-Hearted One, finally succumbed to God, the Creator of Mercy. We are on our way, we are loved, we are thankful.

Recite the standard blessing, followed by today's count: Today is the 1st day of the Omer.

Second blessing: Caring with Involvement

Gevurah sh'b'Chesed (Gev-voo-rah shah bah Chess-ed), "Strength within Grace." Kindness, in the view of the Kabbalah, is on a continuum that stretches from pure strength to pure grace. If you shift too far toward strength, you run the risk of taking over the beneficiary's life. If you shift too far toward grace, you run the risk of disengagement. While some non-Jewish masters see merit in mindless goodness, the Jewish ideal is taking an active role. In the Jewish lexicon, non-involved charity is an oxymoron.

In a way, today's Sefirah points to the difference between a patsy and a donor. A patsy gives a thoughtless handout in response to any whining plea. A donor cares about a cause, or, better, the beneficiaries of a cause; this involves understanding a need and taking action to eliminate the need.

Recite the standard blessing, followed by today's count: Today is the 2nd day of the Omer.

Third blessing: Unconditional Love

Tiferet sh'b'chesed (Tiff-air-et shah bah Chess-ed) proclaims that grace enriched by love produces unconditional love.

The most complete provider of unconditional love in my life was my foster mother, Hubertina (Dina) Janssen. I entered her life during that risk- and threat-filled time now termed the Holocaust. At one point, my family and I were out of options and death was an imminent threat. That's when Dina's husband, Harry, found me and brought me to her like a puppy rescued from the dog pound.

When I arrived unannounced at her doorstep, Dina already was mothering a family of 13, including nine natural-born children. She hardly needed another waif to care for.

Without hesitation, Dina joined *Tiferet* and *Chesed* and locked me into her heart. She committed herself to caring for me and defending my life with hers. She saw this, not as her duty, but as her right. Risk was a distant shadow in Dina's life. Love, on the other hand, was nearby and palpable.

Recite the standard blessing, followed by today's count: Today is the 3rd day of the Omer.

Fourth blessing: Respect for the Other

Netzach sh'b'Chesed (Ney-tzach shah bah Chess-ed) teaches the need to overcome the tendency to see the self as holier than thou. Your favorite *Rebbe*, your revered Master, may have a unique way of creating a holy lifestyle, one that seems just perfect for you. However, that shouldn't make every other life style evil or at least unworthy of attention.

Moment magazine [page 49, February 2000] carried a cartoon showing a candelabra with six of the seven branches twisted off. Just the top branch remained, with the candle holder made to look like a black hat with side curls protruding. The point is that excommunicating people or groups with another belief system is not the Jewish way or the humane way. Each branch of our menorah must be maintained in full splendor and burn with a bright light appreciated and supported by the others.

Recite the standard blessing, followed by today's count: Today is the 4th day of the Omer.

Fifth blessing: Beauty in Grace

Hod sh'b'Chesed (Hoad shah bah Chess-ed) answers the question Nat King Cole asked about Mona Lisa in his song: "Are you warm, are you real, Mona Lisa? Or just a cold and lonely, lovely work of art?"

Seeing Mona Lisa with the eyes of a Kabbalist lets you answer: *She certainly is warm and real, and absolutely neither cold nor lonely. She conveys beauty in grace—splendor without the need to please or impress.* There's a message in that for anyone. Ask the Buddha. In a typical sculpture, his benign image reveals that same beauty in grace without needing to put on airs.

Recite the standard blessing, followed by today's count: Today is the 5th day of the Omer.

Sixth blessing: Common-Sense Grace

Yesod sh'b'Chesed (Yay-soad shah bah Chess-ed) shows us the difference between a gracious act and a gracious person. People can put on a gracious act without being gracious at the core.

You can tell a person who is gracious through and through because that attribute has become part of their personality.

Today's Sefirah also helps distinguish noninvolvement from indifference. Both have an element of withdrawal. If we withdraw emotionally from other people's problems, we become hard and harsh. If we become overly involved in their problems, we become dissipated and scattered. *Yesod sh'b'Chesed* builds a foundation in grace that keeps us from both extremes: Caring, but with gracious boundaries!

Recite the standard blessing, followed by today's count: Today is the 6th day of the Omer.

Seventh blessing: Majestic Guardianship

Malchut sh'b'Chesed (Mawl-choot shah bah Chess-ed) is personified by the eagle, the King of Birds. Jewish lore is filled with imagery using the royal bird as metaphor for the compassion of the King of the World, sheltering His people under His eagle wings; and as rescuing His people on eagle wings to restore them from exile to the Holy Land [Ex. 19:4]

These images were brought to reality in in 1948, when Yemenite Jews had to be rescued from onslaughts by Arab Yemenites after the establishment of the State of Israel. Without time to prepare them for it, Israel sent huge cargo planes to fetch them. The Jewish Yemenites, although quite ready to depart, balked at approaching, much less entering these monstrous apparitions. [See: Tudor Parfitt, *The Road to Redemption: The Jews of the Yemen, 1900-1950.*]

A quick-thinking Israeli airman wisely solved the problem. He cited the "wings of eagles passage," with which the Bible-trained Yemenites were quite familiar. Then, pointing at the cargo planes, he announced: "Look, these are the eagles! Just enter under their wings, as it says in Torah." Reassured, the Yemenites boarded, with their eyes opened to the Majesty in Mercy.

Recite the standard blessing, followed by today's count: Today is the 7th day of the Omer, which completes the first week of the Omer.

The Sabbath of Chesed, Restfulness in Mercy

The Jewish way to be restful about mercy is to stop analyzing and criticizing. Restful grace comes into being by becoming more aware of other people's views, rights, needs, thoughts, and behavior. Lending them respect opens a way to peace, even with contentious, difficult or unpleasant people. You leave self-improvement of others up to them and focus on your own!

SECOND WEEK: GEVURAH

Gevurah (Gev-voo-rah) "heroic strength" points to the fortitude that supports the balanced self and the peaceful world. *Gevurah* implies exercising discipline, especially in dealing with negative influences coming from outside the self as well as seemingly irresistible internal impulses.

The Jewish response to persecution by German Nazis during the Holocaust presents a good example of dealing heroically with massive malevolence. People have asked, *Why didn't you Jews resist the Nazis with force even though we were poorly armed? Even sticks, rocks, Molotov cocktails used in a losing battle are better than going like sheep to slaughter.* The manifold answer lies in the difference between heroic strength versus instinctively hitting back.

• In Stage One, if you believe in law and order, you don't strike back at the first lawless attack you experience. You delay, hoping law and order will return to restrain the attackers. It's a heroically strong position, even though it didn't produce the hoped-for result. In the 1920's, it seemed reasonable to expect protection from Germany's central government against Nazi violence against the Jews, but that government turned out too weak and ineffective.

• When, in Stage Two, you see a dangerous force overwhelm law and order, you still take account of how your actions may affect your family and friends. You restrain the instinctive urge to strike back in order to avoid retribution that the perpetrators might inflict upon others.

• Only in Stage Three, do you spring into defensive action, understanding that nothing else can restrain an irrational but dangerous outside force.

In a major challenge to Jewish resistance, the Nazis set up a huge detention center in the middle of Warsaw, the so-called Warsaw ghetto, expanding it far beyond the former Jewish population of the town. The embattled Jewish leadership hoped for international law and humanitarian aid from abroad to relieve the fear, hunger, and incredibly crowded conditions inside the ghetto. This represented what I call Stage One in response to threat.

In Stage Two, the leadership still restrained armed Jewish resistance to avoid further inflaming the powerful Nazi enemy. The enemy, however, knew no bounds. They caused conditions in the ghetto to worsen and began massive deportations of the inhabitants to concentration camps, meaning death.

Only in Stage Three, when reliance on law and discretion had proven ineffective, did the leadership let ghetto fighters strike back; it resulted in a heroic battle that made rubble of the entire ghetto. Their restraint had been wise, seeing how totally destructive striking back turned out to be.

Eighth blessing: the Peace-Lover's Power

Chesed sh'b'Gevurah (Chess-ed shah bah Gev-voo-rah) is an olive branch taped to a sheathed sword.

A truly strong soldier is a person of peace who serves only to preserve the peace. Conversely, a cold-hearted soldier is a coward who looks to the sword to gain respect but only generates disdain and hate. Similarly, a devoted student spreads modesty and love as he goes through life. The show-off who studies only for self-aggrandizement is soon exposed as a coward and a fraud.

Recite the standard blessing, followed by today's count: Today is the 8th day of the Omer, which makes 1 week and 1 day of the Omer.

Ninth blessing: the Boost of Inner Strength

Gevurah sh'b'Gevurah (Gev-voo-rah shah bah Gev-voo-rah) says that true strength takes spiritual power as well as brawn.

In his seven-week course exploring how the Kabbalah can light up your life [49 Gates of Light, pub. lulu.com 2010], Rabbi Yonassan Gershom points out that the observant servant of the Lord straps tefillin (prayer straps and boxes) to his left arm (or his weaker arm) and on his forehead. He is mindful of the Divine source of his strength (head strap) and aware of his strongest defense, God's strength (arm strap). He is like a Roman soldier with sword held in his right hand and shield strapped to his left—an unbeatable combination.

Recite the standard blessing, followed by today's count: Today is the 9th day of the Omer, which makes one week and two days of the Omer.

Tenth blessing: Beauty Within Strength

Tiferet sh'b'Gevurah (Tiff-air-et shah bah Gev-voo-rah) affirms that a warrior can take on a fight while exhibiting a caring heart, as exemplified by Rachael Denhollander, a former top-level U.S. gymnast.

Time magazine appropriately named her one of its "100 Most Influential People" for 2018 [*Time,* issue of Thursday, April 19, 2018.] She testified in open court against Larry Nassar, a high-level Olympic official accused of violent sexual abuse of teenaged gymnasts. In the same issue, TIME published her reaction to viewing the mountains at Banff National Park in Canada. She said that they represent "enduring, awe-inspiring power combined with serene breath-taking beauty." I can't find better words than hers to describe how elegantly strength and beauty can coexist.

Recite the standard blessing, followed by today's count: Today is the 10th day of the Omer, which makes 1 week and 3 days of the Omer.

Eleventh blessing: Heroic Strength

Netzach sh'b'Gevurah (Ney-tzach shah bah Gev-voo-rah) declares that a person can demonstrate strength without any self-doubt.

Conscious heroes are winners to themselves and their followers. People who are sure of victory ahead never look over their shoulder to see who might be gaining on them, nor do they worry if others momentarily are ahead in the race. They know they are going to come out winners eventually, no matter what numbers are currently flashing on the Scoreboard.

Recite the standard blessing, followed by today's count: Today is the 11th day of the Omer, which makes 1 week and 4 days of the Omer.

Twelfth blessing: The Splendid Understatement

Hod sh'b'Gevurah (Hoad shah bah Gev-voo-rah) proclaims that strength is splendor. It reminds me of "Splendid China," a theme park near Orlando, Florida, set in an attractive, natural environment. The park presents the strongest architectural wonders of China, recreated in only one-tenth their actual size. They are beautiful, strong understatements of splendor.

Recite the standard blessing, followed by today's count: Today is the 12th day of the Omer, which makes 1 week and 5 days of the Omer.

Thirteenth blessing: The Foundation of Strength

Yesod sh'b'Gevurah (Yay-soad shah bah Gev-voo-rah) is the spiritual pediment that holds up the statue of pure strength. Think of the statue of David by Michaelangelo and you see pure strength and power.

Then contrast that with the strength of Abraham, our Founding Father; his strength can't be modeled in marble, because how would you picture spiritual strength?

Abraham's foundation of strength is his spiritual connection with a Higher Power linked with a strong moral sense, the sense of what is Right. This is illustrated by his expedition to rescue his nephew Lot, as related in Scripture [Gen. 14].

When Abraham hears that Lot was taken prisoner, he gathers a small band of warriors to assail an alliance of the strongest kings of the neighborhood, one of whom holds Lot captive. Abraham tastes victory because of his moral rectitude and faith in God, not principally because of overwhelming physical or numerical strength.

"Free the captive" is the moral lesson of this legend, which has become the battle-cry of Jewish practice. God is not quoted in the Bible as spelling out this rule, even though it is expounded on extensively in other Jewish literature; Abraham's foundation of strength clearly says it all.

Recite the standard blessing, followed by today's count: Today is the 13th day of the Omer, which makes 1 week and 6 days of the Omer.

Fourteenth blessing: The Rein on Reign

Malchut sh'b'Gevurah (Mawl-chóót shah bah Gev-voo-rah) connects the homonyms rein and reign to tell us that we must impose limits on absolute power.

Although, we are captains of our ship and masters of our fate, we still should be aware of and responsive to the needs of others. That's the message that the Prophet Nathan conveyed to King David whenever the latter overstepped the bounds of his power. Nathan conveyed that your ability to get done what you want to get done must be limited by the realization that you shouldn't do everything you want.

Another dimension of Malchut sh'b'Gevurah illustrates that you should carefully choose causes into which you put your energy. On the one hand, you can err by pursuing a lost cause that doesn't fit into our world. Conversely, you can err by stopping the pursuit of a worthwhile ideal that the rest of the world won't immediately accept. Understanding the rein on reign can help you make the needed distinction.

Recite the standard blessing, followed by today's count: Today is the 14th day of the Omer, which makes two complete weeks of the Omer.

The Sabbath of Gevurah, Respite of the Strong

Rest is built into life. The Sabbath practices of Jewish tradition guide a basic human need into a fixed channel. Experiments show that even the brightest, strongest, healthiest people must have rest, or else their life degenerates into illusion and disorientation.

What about the professional student? If you learn in Yeshivah all week, what do you do on Shabbat? The Talmud contains a morality tale about a great scholar, Rabbi Yehuda ben Chiyya, who was so entranced by a new inspiration from the Torah that he forgot to go home for the Sabbath. The story goes that "his fire went out" and he died [BT Ketubot 62b.]

My sense is that the professional student must stop studying on Shabbat to spend time with his family (as the Talmudic story suggests) and tend to his body. I think there is a message in the stereotype of the professional student who is bent, pudgy, and out of shape. As the Romans used to advise: *Mens sana en corpora sano*: you need a strong body to support a strong mind. Those with strength in their studies must also develop bodily strength, and they should consider making their Sabbath into a *Shabbat* of Gevurah. Or else, their fire, also, may go out.

THIRD WEEK: TIFERET

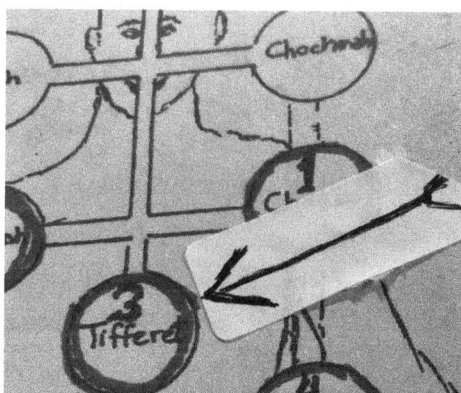

Tiferet (Tiff-ay-ret) literally means "beauty," but often is identified with "heart," as if to say "Beautiful Heart." *Tiferet* expresses centered-ness and sits at the center of the Tree of Life. Kabbalists say, it's the place where the Divine of the World Above meets the Mundane of the World Below.

The human heart is not only the center from which life blood flows, but it's the center of the spirit that infuses our soul. It sends sustenance to each cell and brings a blessing to every atom of our spirit. *Tiferet* holds together what is below so that it doesn't drift away from what is above. *Tiferet* keeps us alive spiritually and overcomes whatever pulls us away from the center.

Fifteenth blessing: Mercy of Heart

Chesed sh'b'Tiferet (Chess-ed shah ba *Tiff-ay-ret)* echoes the prayer: "Purify our hearts to serve God in Truth." It reemphasizes that with resentment in our heart, we cannot be spiritual. We must show mercy to ourselves and others to cause our spirit to be fully functional and active. We cannot reach God until our heart is at peace.

When I give lectures about the Holocaust, I often am asked whether I have forgiven the Germans for letting the Nazis take over their government and then launch a massive genocide. I find my best answer in *Chesed sh'b'Tiferet*. I can't work on my spiritual self until my heart is freed from visions of revenge. In freeing my heart, forgiveness almost becomes irrelevant. Rancor fades from my heart, and I let the Germans worry about the burden of living down the ignominy of the Holocaust.

Recite the standard blessing, followed by today's count: Today is the 15th day of the Omer, which makes 2 weeks and 1 day of the Omer.

Sixteenth blessing: Strength of Heart

Gevurah sh'b'Tiferet (Gev-voo-rah shah ba Tiff-ay-ret) says that the more centered you become, the stronger you must work to stay centered. We admire the adept who can not only inspire others with his spiritual strength but also maintain his own internal balance.

Remaining centered is difficult. To maintain the balance that supports his mastery, a Guru can't let the adulation he receives go to his head.

Furthermore, the balanced adept learns to adapt—he can't just blindly pursue his mission. The story of Jonah, the off-balance prophet, illustrates this point.

In the book of Jonah, God commands him to prophesy the doom of Nineveh. Nineveh was the capital of Assyria, so Jonah's assignment was risky. It was like sending Martin Luther King to the Kremlin during the height of the Cold War to tell Krushchev to get right with God, or else.

Jonah was told to say: "Another 40 days, and Nineveh will be history." He pronounced the evil decree and then sat outside town under a carob tree and waited for the minarets of Nineveh to come tumbling down. Instead, the king and the people repented.

God forgave the people of Nineveh, but Jonah couldn't adjust. He bitterly protested to God that he had staked his life and his reputation on this perilous mission. Now his reputation was ruined because his prophesy didn't come true. (Actually, it did, but not until later. The

Assyrians hardly became role models of piety and neighborliness, and about 50 years later—606 BCE—the Babylonians came visiting to crumble Nineveh into rubble, as predicted.)

Jonah lost his power as a prophet because he forgot that the repentance of the citizenry of Nineveh was his true mission, not his desire to shine as a prophet. The lesson is that leaders should focus on staying balanced, not on becoming a star.

Recite the standard blessing, followed by today's count: Today is the 16th day of the Omer, which makes 2 weeks and 2 days of the Omer.

Seventeenth blessing: Our Magnetic Core

Tiferet sh'b'tiferet (Tiff-ay-ret shah ba Tiff-ay-ret) pulls together love, life, and spirit, so that we are truly at peace and in balance. When life events drain our spirit, Tiferet sh'b'Tiferet can pull our spirit back to center. We need to put effort into keeping the core of our hearts "magnetic," so that our heart stays locked onto love and spirit.

Recite the standard blessing, followed by today's count: Today is the 17th day of the Omer, which makes 2 weeks and 3 days of the Omer.

Eighteenth blessing: The Spiritual Medal of Honor

Netzach sh'b'Tiferet (Ney-tzach shah bah Tiff-ay-ret) in action brings your life into control so that you can be fully centered. It gives you a sense of honor, of victory, of getting a spiritual Medal of Honor that says, *You deserve a medal today for fighting off distraction—of dealing effectively with the sticks, stones, and spread sheets in the world.*

The *Netzach* type of Victory comes to play in the Scriptural story of Jacob having to confront Esau [Gen. 33]. The story opens as Jacob is returning home to the land of his fathers, which his twin-brother Esau is currently administering. Jacob finds the prospect of the encounter daunting; he hasn't seen or heard from Esau since, years earlier, he had to flee from an incensed Esau because Jacob had fleeced him out of his birthright.

Jacob brings with him a sizable group of fighters, but he intuits that military confrontation isn't an effective way to settle with his brother. He spends a restless night wrestling with the topic, which Scripture call his wrestling with "an angel." Jacob wakes up in the morning with a sore hip, a symbol of his internal victory, for which he gets awarded a new name, Israel (a "spiritual medal of honor"). His dream prompts Israel to send his brother a conciliatory message and generous gifts instead of a challenge. He attained true victory emerging from the heart.

Recite the standard blessing, followed by today's count: Today is the 18th day of the Omer, which makes 2 weeks and 4 days of the Omer.

Nineteenth blessing: The Call to Joy

Hod sh'b'Tiferet (Hoad shah ba Tiff-ay-ret) says, *Enjoy yourself, it's later than you think.* It says, don't focus so hard and relentlessly on the spiritual path that joy goes out the window.

Look at your progress and exclaim: "Wonderful! Now, how much more deeply can I enjoy the beauty in the world if I walk the spiritual path!"

The Holocaust-era movie *Life is Beautiful* shows how love and optimism can continue under extremely adverse circumstances. Its theme is: If you are balanced and together, life is beautiful for you no matter what happens in your world.

Recite the standard blessing, followed by today's count: Today is the 19th day of the Omer, which makes 2 weeks and 5 days of the Omer.

Twentieth blessing: The Stable Heart

Yesod sh'b'Tiferet (Yay-soad shah ba Tiff-ay-ret), reminds us that the best balance is unstable unless it rests on a firm foundation. The heart needs to feel secure before it can shine forth in beauty. Well-anchored, the heart feels at home and in its place, right where it should be.

The Life of Doña Gracia of Nasi (1510-1569) illustrates that point. She already was a rich and generous Jewish woman when she lived in Spain under the shadow of the Inquisition in Sixteenth Century Europe. After she moved to Turkey--out of the reach of the Inquisitor—she was at her most influential. The protection of the Sultan provided her the firm foundation from which to more effectively endow the needy, protect the persecuted, and promote Jewish culture.

Recite the standard blessing, followed by today's count: Today is the 20th day of the Omer, which makes 2 weeks and 6 days of the Omer.

Twenty-first blessing: The Heart's Message

Malchut sh'b'Tiferet (Mawl-chóót shah ba Tiff-ay-ret) is a blessing that helps you overcome the tendency to just remain still when in balance. It says: *Actively promote spiritual growth; don't just sit on it.*

In Jewish religious study, the practice of "Each one teach one" is standard procedure. Students typically learn in pairs, and often a more advanced student is paired with a student of lesser accomplishments. The system benefits both. Even a great master, finds that he, too, enjoys and learns from paired study.

Recite the standard blessing, followed by today's count: Today is the 21th day of the Omer, which makes three entire weeks of the Omer.

The Sabbath of Tiferet, the Holiness of Time

The Beautiful Heart of Shabbat is *time*. Rabbi Abraham Joshua Heschel (January 11, 1907-December 23, 1972), the great Master of our day and age, explains this at great length in his book, "The Sabbath." He points out that at the center of other religions we typically find a place: A holy mountain, an obelisk, or a huge cathedral. In contrast, the center of Judaism is the sanctification of time.

Rabbi Heschel points out that the Jewish legend about the creation of the world doesn't end with God appointing a holy **location** at which people could worship and give thanks. He appointed a holy **day** for the purpose. Time is made sacred and the holiest time of all in Jewish practice is the Sabbath--that's the message of the Sabbath of Tiferet.

FOURTH WEEK: Blessings of Netzach, Celebrating Mastery

Netzach (Nay-tsach), translated as "Victory," should not be understood in a triumphalist sense. In a spiritual sense, Victory isn't victory over somebody else; instead, it refers to mastery over the negative side of the self. Even that spiritual victory shouldn't give rise to an overly glowing feeling of inner satisfaction.

Symbolically, *Netzach* celebrates the benefits of inner purity. Traditionally, that sense comes to the fore in the Book of Maccabees, which relates the miraculous victory of "purity" over hedonism (a deuterocanonical book, cited as "1 Maccabees").

In the sense that *Netzach* is the theme of that story, it points to God as the Power in the Universe that allows good to triumph over evil. It intimates that the world would not continue to run if God hadn't set up the Power of Good as ultimately victorious.

Netzach also raises the intriguing side question, *Why do we sometimes call the Deity* Adonai Tsevaot *(Ah-doan-ah-ee Tza-vah-oat)*? Translated literally, this means "Leader of Armies." That leads us to ask, "At the head of what army does God march?"

We can find an answer in the Book of Samuel [I Sam. 6]. In that story, a barren woman, named Hannah, addresses a heart-rending plea to God as "Lord of Hosts" to "open her womb" and beget a son. In that context, she couldn't have been thinking of God as a Major General! More likely, she was addressing God as *Master of the Host of Disembodied Souls*. Her plea then means *Please God, let go of one of the myriads of souls, and let it incorporate as my future baby son.*" Scripture supports that interpretation, saying that Hannah's plea was bountifully answered. Not only did she beget a son, but he also grew up to become the prophet Samuel who promulgated her story for posterity.

Twenty-second blessing: Mercy in Victory

Chesed sh'b'Netzach (Chess-ed shah ba Ney-tzach) says that the enlightened victor should ensure peace beyond victory.

Compare, for example, the follow-up to victory of the victorious forces in World War I with that in World War II. After hostilities ended in 1918, the Allies exacted severe reparations, the opposite of what *Chesed sh'b'netzach* would indicate. That unenlightened demand following victory helped provoke a deep depression, in which the evil of National Socialism took root and then grew into the horrid excesses of the Holocaust.

By contrast, the victors instituted a Marshall Plan when World War II ended in 1945, which helped the vanquished foe back to regaining its economic feet. In both Germany and Japan, support from the victors led to the first truly democratic government in their history, and both economies blossomed into an economic miracle.

To put *Chesed sh'b'Netzach* on a personal scale, when you want to conquer some bad habit, cursing the vanquished part of the self is not merciful and isn't healthy. Great masters often tell with humor and grace about the escapades of their youth. And if they counsel people, the Masters are never judgmental, always kind. It is a good model to follow.

Recite the standard blessing, followed by today's count: Today is the 22nd day of the Omer, which makes 3 weeks and 1 day of the Omer.

Twenty-third blessing: Strength in Victory

Gevurah sh'b'Netzach (Gev-voo-rah shah ba Ney-tzach) asks a riddle: *Do you need power when you have Victory?*

Of course, the answer is, **Yes**. You need strength in victory to restrain yourself from lording it over the vanquished. The Bible instructs Jewish armies to spare the trees of the enemy even if uprooting them would make victory easier; and to deal fairly with women taken from the vanquished party. The more others are at your mercy, the more inner strength you need to act with restraint and dignity.

On the personal level, if you reach mastery over the weaker parts of yourself, you must not gloat or boast. When you become a true hero of self-mastery, you use strength to attain balance and maintain perspective. You blend into your environment and look like you belong beautifully right where you are. That takes true strength.

Recite the standard blessing, followed by today's count: Today is the 23rd day of the Omer, which makes 3 weeks and 2 days of the Omer.

Twenty-fourth blessing: Balance within Victory

Tiferet sh'b'Netzach (Tiff-ay-ret shah ba Ney-tzach) demonstrates the kind of victory that comes to victors who have a Beautiful Heart.

You can understand that by comparing two stories of two celebrities. One story, is an imaginary composite of corporate take-over stories in the Wall Street Journal, in which the victor takes over the assets of a rival Corporation. The other is the famous tale by Mark Twain titled "A Connecticut Yankee in King Arthur's Court."

The composite "take-over" story ends with the victorious Chairman of the Board firing the leadership of the corporation that is being swallowed up. When successful, the take-over results in a huge increase in the value of the victorious company's stocks, and the Chairman is rewarded with a huge bonus, which he uses to buy the biggest, fanciest yacht available on the market.

In our analysis, Mark Twain's story of the Connecticut Yankee illustrates how proper balance within victory works. The Yankee as Noble Knight, sitting upright on his steed with a firm grip on his lance, fearlessly faces the mean, scary dragon. Being victorious, the Connecticut Yankee is feted by the people of England and knighted by the famous king Arthur. He uses his fame to win the heart of the Beautiful Princess, who marries him, and they live happily together ever after.

When you compare the two stories, you see that the Chairman of the Board has a personal victory but hardly evidences a Beautiful Heart. The Connecticut Yankee as Noble Warrior also has a personal victory, but does so preserving and evidencing a Beautiful Heart. **Recite the standard blessing,** followed by today's count: Today is the 24th day of the Omer, which makes 3 weeks and 3 days of the Omer.

Twenty-fifth blessing: Stricture vs. Structure

Netzach sh'b'Netzach (Ney-tzach shah ba Ney-tzach) holds that Victory comes to its own only when the victor is at peace with himself. The peaceful victor doesn't have to prove anything. He allows the seeds of victory to sprout into beautiful flower fields.

The victor able to maintain stricture over structure is able to set boundaries for himself that ensure inner and outer peace; and he assures others that he can bring this same peace to the outer world. His strength is directed against evil, against distractions, and against invasion of privacy.

Recite the standard blessing, followed by today's count: Today is the 25th day of the Omer, which makes 3 weeks and 4 days of the Omer.

Twenty-sixth blessing: Accomplishment Without Guilt

Hod sh'b'Netzach (Hoad shah ba Ney-tzach) tells you that you have every right to enjoy your accomplishments and that you fully deserve what you have created. It is victory without guilt, enjoyment without static.

The static to avoid is the constant self-criticism that sometimes rings in my ears. It's as if a little crow is perched like a gremlin on my shoulder, ready to disparage any victory. When I accomplish something powerful, the discouraging bird likes to crow: "What's so great about that? You could have done it better, sooner, faster, more elegantly. Caw-caw."

Hod sh' b'Netzach can calm that static by substituting a comforting canary that coos: "Good job, fellow. You used your noodle and accomplished something for yourself. You deserve this. And more!" That kind of message is essential to fully savoring victory.

Recite the standard blessing, followed by today's count: Today is the 26th day of the Omer, which makes 3 weeks and 5 days of the Omer.

Twenty-seventh blessing: Ideals vs. Action

Yesod sh' b'Netzach (Yes shah ba Ney-tzach) says that a solid victory needs to be based on a solid ideal. It suggests that you should define and refine the reasons why you want victory before you sharpen your lance and saddle your horse. Ask yourself, is the prize worth the effort and the cost?

Then, ponder the possible disturbances your victory might create in your community and in your environment. Sure, it may be necessary to face the disapproval of others. However, *Yesod sh' b'Netzach* encourages you to assess the overall impact of victory before you go into battle.

Recite the standard blessing, followed by today's count: Today is the 27th day of the Omer, which makes 3 weeks and 6 days of the Omer.

Twenty-eighth blessing: The Majesty of Wisdom

Malchut sh'b'Netzach (Mawl-choot shah ba Ney-tzach) illustrates the benefit of using royal power wisely instead of imposing an arbitrary decree.

It comes to the fore in the story of how King Solomon adjudicates a case of competing mothers who battle for the custody of a baby. It appears in a Scriptural passage [Kings 3:16-28], that relates how King Solomon uses psychology to resolve this case.

After Solomon hears the mothers present their claims, he suggests cutting the baby in half, so each petitioner can take home an equal, fair share."

Of course, Solomon presupposes that the true mother would rather give up the baby than have it cut in half, while the pretender, in spite, would agree to the verdict.

And so it happened. The true mother bursts into tears and drops her claim while the pretender accepts the King's first ruling. Next, Salomon changes his verdict, awarding the whole baby to the rightful mother, thereby demonstrating the efficacious use of royal power!

Recite the standard blessing, followed by today's count: Today is the 28th day of the Omer, which makes four entire weeks of the Omer.

The 28th day of the Omer also can be celebrated as a Second Passover. The Torah (Numbers 9:10) instituted this second chance for observing the holiday, originally just for people who unavoidably missed making the required sacrifice for Passover at the regular time. Four us today, we can use this day to regain the joys of Passover, as by eating Matzot or by any reminder that we like.

The Sabbath of Netzach, Celebrating Victory

To interpret *Shabbat b'Netzach,* I picture two different teams winning a championship athletic competition. The first team has a positive Netzach response. Upon attaining the championship for their team, the members run up to the losing side, and meet them with a comradely response: "Good game, fellows! You played well, and at one point in the game we almost thought you were going to win. We enjoyed your able and effective teamwork."

By contrast, the winning team exhibiting a negative Netzach response totally snubs the opposing team, yelling: "Look!! Did you see how we stuck it to these chumps?

In a broader context, the Sabbath of Victory, challenges participants from both sides to access a secure sense of themselves. With positive spirit coming from the core of their being, they can dispel animosity or resentment in their world—any lingering negativity, anywhere.

FIFTH WEEK: HOD

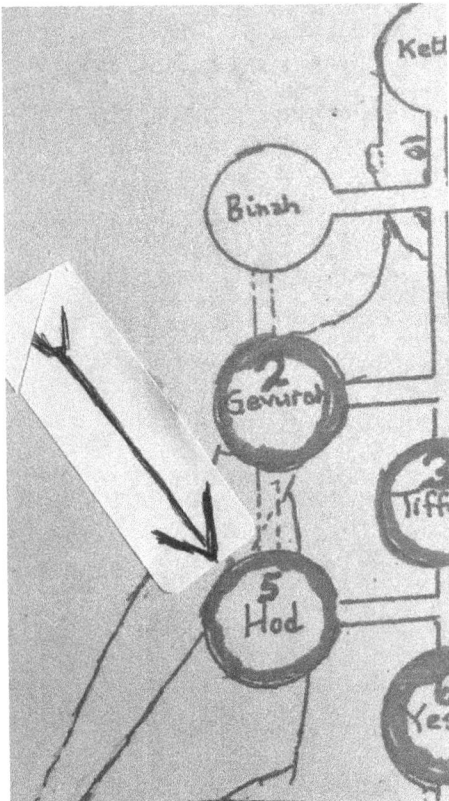

Hod (Hoad), "Splendor" renders me a deep personal significance. It takes my mind to the magnificent ceremony prepared for the investiture of the first cultic High Priest of Judaism, as described in Scripture [Lev. 10]. Performed before all the former slaves camped out in the Sinai Desert, the ceremony prepared for Aaron, Moses's brother, was deliberately designed to overawe all onlookers with maximum splendor.

After spending chapters of Scripture on preparations for that great day, Torah, very briefly describes how the ceremony was interrupted by an unscheduled, awesome performance by Aaron's two eldest sons, Nadav and Avihu, who were supposed to have only minor, supportive roles. Scripture just states that they "offered unauthorized fire."

Actually, their fireworks must have been so audacious and impressive that the onlookers gasped in disbelief, and God was so incensed at their audacity that God struck the two young men dead on the spot. To maintain the impact of the official ceremony, God sternly and absolutely insisted that Aaron complete the day's observance as scheduled without time out to mourn his sons or exhibit any troubled emotion in public.

With this disrupted splendor before my eyes, I still re-experience the pressure I myself once felt when called upon to perform publicly but stoically soon after my own son's death.

The splendiferous event that preceded his death, highlighted the ceremonial race performed by the U.S. track and field teams qualifying to represent America at the Summer Olympics scheduled for 2004 in Athens, Greece. An unforeseen and still unexplained challenge caused Albert to fall behind the leading competitors in his event, even though Albert had outstripped all the rest in their first few laps.

Narrowly missing the medals awarded the top performers made Albert feel humiliated, ashamed, and deeply disappointed. Two days after the race, Albert dodged his friends and teammates, and, blaming himself while standing at the top of a gorge, he snapped emotionally and jumped off into the depths to his death.

Not surprisingly, news of Albert's suicide was shattering to his fellow athletes; they found themselves asking, *Is winning truly more important than life?* Leading sports reporters actually peppered me with such questions, and in response, the team psychologist, spiritual advisors, and Olympic Center managers asked me to help plan and arrange a ceremony at which the Olympic team could openly express and deal with feelings like "there but for the Grace of God go I."

Preparations for the Olympics went on, but I felt the same lack of support from God that Aaron must have felt at his investiture. I started to wander the hills around the Olympic Training Center, and I cried out in the words of Psalm 121, "I lift up my eyes to the mountains (and plead) whence and from where will my consolation come?" I still struggle with this question, and I dissolve in tears at every anniversary of Albert's death (February 14). I look elsewhere than in Scripture's Leviticus 14 for reassurance that despite all its challenges, life still is beautiful.

Twenty-ninth blessing: Compassion in Kindness

Chesed sh' b'Hod (Chess-ed shah ba Hoad) teaches that kindness should be judged by the outcome, not by the intent. If you mean to do a kindness and it feels like an assault by the recipient, then you must apologize and change your behavior, no matter how noble your motivation. When there is grace and compassion within splendor, the gift enables the receiver to

feel love and the giver to feel true satisfaction

Recite the standard blessing, followed by today's count: Today is the 29th day of the Omer which makes 4 weeks and 1 day of the Omer.

Thirtieth blessing: The Power of Charisma

Gevurah sh' b'Hod (Gev-voo-rah shah ba Hoad) is the Power of Attraction, which is the Power of Charisma. The Talmud contains a legend about the encounter of two paragons of charisma. One is Rabbi Yochanan, a noted scholar and "the most beautiful man in Pumbedita." The other is Resh Lakish, a strongman, a Robin Hood of Israel, who at the start of the story is fearlessly leading a band of bandits [BT Bava Metzia 84]. Attracted by each other's charisma, each champion started challenging the other.

Said Resh Lakish: "May your beauty be for women."
Countered Rabbi Yochanan: "May your strength be for Torah. If you turn aside from your ways, I will give you my sister, who is more beautiful than I."

On impulse, Resh Lakish accepted the challenge from Rabbi Yochanan. What the bandit didn't know is that Rabbi Yochanan's "beautiful sister" was the Torah. When he caught on to Rabbi Yochanan's metaphor, he stayed the course, became the Rabbi's disciple and close friend, and gained a great name as a Torah scholar.

Resh Lakish came to understand that his charisma derived from strength and beauty both of which are God-given.

Recite the standard blessing, followed by today's count: Today is the 30st day of the Omer, which makes 4 weeks and 2 days of the Omer.

Thirty-first blessing: Disciplined Celebration

Tiferet sh' b'Hod (Tiff-air-et shah bah Hoad) is the balance you look for in planning an elegant party in your home as opposed to a bawdy bash in a bar. In making up your invitation list, you must go beyond selecting people who would enjoy and support the party theme. You would balance the invitations to include introverts and extroverts, fun people and thoughtful people, leaders and followers.

Similarly, the activities you'd plan would be balanced: Learning games and fun games; games of skill and games of chance; activities with motion and quiet pastimes. The same would go for the menu: Meat and tofu; veggies and pasta; sweet pies and ripe fruit for dessert. Planning is central to achieve a balanced outcome that pleases most of the people involved.

Recite the standard blessing, followed by today's count: Today is the 31st day of the Omer, which makes 4 weeks and 3 days of the Omer.

Thirty-second blessing: Celebrating Just Deserts

Netzach sh'b'hod (Ney-tzach shah ba Hoad) prods us to enjoy the splendor of our lives with abandon. With our eyes glancing over our shoulders at the Victory we have attained, we are free to shout for joy, sing hallelujah, and jubilate: "Ashreynu ma tov chelkeynu, ma nayim goralenu, ma yaffa yerushateynu" [Chasidic song of praise] *Let us be happy with our good breaks, our pleasant fate, and our lucky stars.*

Recite the standard blessing, followed by today's count: Today is the 32nd day of the Omer, which makes 4 weeks and 4 days of the Omer.

Thirty-third blessing: Unlimited Splendor

Hod sh'b'Hod (Hoad shah ba Hoad) is the glory of everything, the call to enjoy the beauty of nature, the innate splendor in life. It is a resting place in the counting of the Omer, a time to catch our breath. Even traditions that see the Omer as a period of mourning for our many losses recognize the splendor and joy of the 33rd day.

At its roots, Day 33 was the wheat growers' moment of truth. If the crop was doing well, they could breathe a sigh of relief, because they believed that once wheat made it safely to Day 33, a plentiful harvest was virtually assured.

For this reason, we have come to observe Day 33 as a holiday called *Lag b 'Omer.* The name stems from the Classical Hebrew practice of having the letters of the alphabet do double duty as numerals. (In this system, the letter *Lamed* is 30, and the letter *Gimmel* is 3, so that LG represents 33. With a vowel sound added, LG becomes the "LaG" of the Omer.)

We customarily celebrate the holiday with picnics and outdoor games, in remembrance of a bittersweet legend. During the time of the Second Temple when the Romans occupied Judea, they forbade Jewish study. However, they admired games of skill and military drill.

To fool the Romans into letting them study, the rabbis and their students went outdoors with bats and balls and bows and arrows. Once there, they put down their bats and all, ready to pick them up again if they heard strangers approach.

With all that sports equipment lying around, the young students must have played some games and sports anyway. That's what we do today. We take a break from study, work, and meditation and go outdoors to picnic and play.

Recite the standard blessing, followed by today's count: Today is the 33rd day of the Omer, which makes 4 weeks and 5 days of the Omer.

Thirty-fourth blessing: The Smile of Wisdom

Yesod sh'b'hod (Yay-soad shah ba Hoad) points to the difference between real gold and fool's gold. Both glitter, but only one has true monetary value. Similarly, a smile can be the expression of splendor in an integrated person or the empty posturing of a fool.

The smile of wisdom reveals inner peace and wisdom. It warms the observer's heart. A fool's smile, on the other hand, is manipulative and the hallmark of cheap public relations. It doesn't reach the heart of the observer. So the smile of wisdom in *Yesod sh'b'hod* urges us to respond only to the wise smile—not the fake put-on smirk!

Recite the standard blessing, followed by today's count: Today is the 34th day of the Omer, which makes 4 weeks and 6 days of the Omer.

Thirty-fifth blessing: The Outreach of Greatness

Malchut sh'b'hod (Mawl-choot shah ba Hoad) examines how demonstrating splendor in public—revealing and sharing leadership and charisma—poses a great personal risk. The Master who shines *and* acts publicly in the world tends to attract both enthusiastic enemies *and* fanatic followers—and he accepts the risk in service of a higher cause.

Conversely, a leader without *Malchut sh'b'hod* stays in his castle and fortifies the walls and deepens the moat. He is a Slobodan Milosevich or a Saddam Hussein, and they seem to survive beyond all expectations. Conversely, a leader who is blessed with true *Malchut sh'b'hod* becomes a Jesus, a Martin Luther King, a Rabbi Akiba, a Gandhi, all lives that were tragically and brutally cut short. This outcome shows the sad truth that *Malchut* with *Hod* poses a risk. Truly charismatic leaders are aware of the risk but are willing to reach out nonetheless. Let us pray for their reward in Heaven.

Recite the standard blessing, followed by today's count: Today is the 35th day of the Omer, which makes five complete weeks of the Omer.

The Sabbath of Hod, Mystical Splendor

Hebrew assigns gender to its nouns. Day and Holiday are masculine. Sabbath, by contrast, is feminine. She is called a bride, a queen, a mystical beauty.

Although Judaism tends to stay away from personification, in this case, the Kabbalists of Sefad invested *Kabbalat Shabbat* (Welcoming of the Sabbath) with great drama. They walked from their place of worship to the edge of the city on Friday afternoon. Precisely at the hour of official nightfall and the start of Shabbat, they would start a parade into town as if they were escorting a corporeal queen, greatly beloved by her people. If we can capture that image, we will have gained access to the Sabbath in her full splendor.

SIXTH WEEK: YESOD

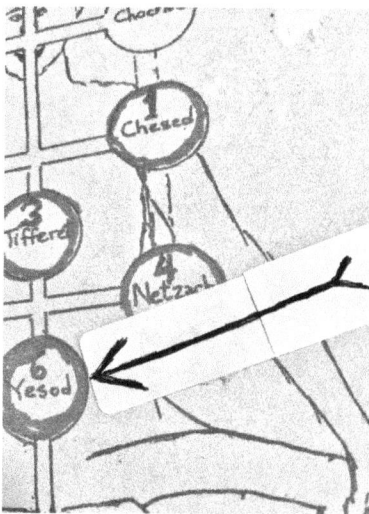

Yesod (Yay-soad), "foundation," refers to the root system of the Tree of Life that holds up and feeds everything above it. With *Yesod* I am free to visualize, to dream, to wish—secure in the knowledge that my wishes will come true. In Yesod, I find permission to use all my creative powers, and for Yesod, to give out my thanks for collecting the fruits of my wishing.

It is remarkable that Jewish masters have put a high value on creative endeavor, when the standard advice of Eastern mystics is to stop doing. The Jewish view holds that human beings are co-creators with God. And God's creation of the world is seen as an act of love, quite different from the cataclysmic creation stories of other cultures.

Jewish masters say that if we keep our spirits attuned, we will do creative work that brings us closer to God. The Jewish adept counsels us to work hard and then rest wholeheartedly on a regular schedule every week because rest and study are rewards for good creative work.

The creative energy of *Yesod* also is identified with sexual power and creation of new life, especially new life that leads to salvation. Actually, Jewish lore has two such stories, providing great truths from more than one angle.

In the first of the two related stories in the Bible [Gen. 38], which is rich in detail, sexual seduction is seen in a positive light. In this story, the heroine, Tamar, enforces the practice of the *levir* (providing an heir to the first-born male in the family). She uses her wiles to force the patriarch Judah to provide her with an heir. Through this seductive work by Tamar, a son is born who connects the Abrahamic line to our Ideal King, King David, who in turn is seen as the progenitor of the Messiah.

The Torah strays chronologically by putting the second of the seduction stories virtually cheek to jowl [Gen. 39:7-20] with the first. Here sexual seduction is put in a negative light. The heroine, identified only as Mrs. Potiphar, uses her wiles to distract God's servant, Joseph.

Even though her seductive behavior is deplored, it still is seen, willy-nilly, as promoting God's plan for the Jews. Joseph, by distancing himself from the sexy Mrs. Potiphar, is rewarded by becoming perhaps the most powerful Jewish politician in history. And a lesser-known tradition honors this politician by picturing the Messiah as the "Son (descendant) of Joseph."

Thirty-sixth blessing: Grace in Judgment

Chesed sh' b'Yesod (Chess-ed shah bah Yay-soad) brings us to the immense Jewish preoccupation with numbers, in particular with numbers involved with a census. Some say a superstition is behind this—the sense that being assigned a number strips the soul from its natural protection.

In Hebrew, the same word root, *Zachar,* covers both the word "male" (the unit to be counted) and the word "remember." The implication is that we need to remember each person making up the count, not just the totality of the numbers counted.

Even in today's non-superstitious climate, we still hate just being a number. Calling me by my Social Security Number takes away my dignity as a person and opens me up to invasion of privacy. Sensitive to this unwillingness to call people just by a number, the *gabbai* in charge of certifying a *Minyan* (the Jewish group-prayer quorum), traditionally counts the congregation as "Not one, not two . . .," etc.

Anyhow, the Bible relates that this resistance to numbering was at its superstitious peak when Moses first suggested doing a headcount [Ex. 30:12]. He wanted a working figure on how many able-bodied men he could muster as soldiers, and he declared that the census was demanded straight from God.

Resistance to the count, however, was so high that people didn't even bend to a demand from On High. So Moses had an inspiration. He required each draftable male to pay a half-shekel tax. Instead of counting heads, Moses now could count half-shekels. In this way, he not only got the numbers he wanted, he also accrued a war chest of shekels to buy the latest armaments.

The issue comes up again later in Torah, at the start of the Fourth Book of Moses, which, significantly, is called the Book of Numbers [Num. 1:1]. The (apparent) repetition lends emphasis to the seriousness and importance accorded to taking a census.

King David, the other great hero of Judaic lore, also had census problems [I Samuel 24]. Almost immediately after he ordered a census, an epidemic broke out in the land, killing 70,000 inhabitants. Obviously, the people blamed the epidemic on the census and David almost lost his throne over this incident.

The moral of these stories is that you need to see behind the number to see a person's soul. The Bible calls the half-shekel census tax "a ransom to the Lord." This rather mysterious appellation points to the Mercy in Yesod.

When dealing with numbering anything other than humans, Jews are positively in love with numbers. For example, we tease meaning out of the spelling of words by looking up their numerical equivalent. Take the Hebrew word for "life," *Chai* (Chah-hee). Its numerical value is eighteen, seeing that it is spelled with a *Yud* (10) and a *Chet* (8). Life carries a high value, so 18 is seen as a propitious number. Gifts of money often are made in multiples of 18.

So the 36th day of the Omer is double-lucky. Jewish lore even holds that God preserves the world by judging with grace—he lets the world stumble on thanks to the merit of 36 saintly people who walk with grace and rectitude.

Recite the standard blessing, followed by today's count: Today is the 36th day of the Omer, which makes 5 weeks and 1 day of the Omer.

Thirty-seventh blessing: Constructive Peace

Gevurah sh' b'Yesod (Gev-voo-rah shah bah Yay-soad) says that an effectively working society is based on peace. No people can better attest to that then the Jews, who, until recently, have lived in other people's countries, caught in the crossfire of other people's bellicosity.

Unfortunately, even now, where Jews can live in their own country, lack of a constructive peace takes money that could be better spent on social programs. Israel spent around $15 billion annually on defense in recent years because even there, Jewish people are targeted by bellicose forces.

Peace clearly is the foundation of Israel's national strength and remains the Jewish people's greatest hope. Traditional Hebrew prayers call God *"Oseh ha-Shalom"* Maker of Peace," and call Peace itself "His most precious gift."

Recite the standard blessing, followed by today's count: Today is the 37th day of the Omer, which makes 5 weeks and 2 days of the Omer.

Thirty-eighth blessing: Moral Balance

Tiferet sh'b'Yesod (Tiff-ay-ret shah bah Yay-sod) says my foundation must be level and balanced. In personal, practical terms that means weak moral values will fall like poorly constructed buildings when an earthquake hits.

Let's examine telling the truth as a key moral value because for me it's a major challenge; I am a Libra who believes in Moral Relativity. To give myself minimum moral wiggle room, I have resolved never to lie to benefit myself, not even just to make myself more comfortable in social situations.

I look for wiggle room, however, when it comes to making others comfortable, heal an injury, or save a life. In these cases, I think I don't violate the message of *Tiferet sh'b'Yesod*. However, I'm not every man, and every person needs to measure his own actions against that foundational message—one that's such a valuable guide to moral living.

Recite the standard blessing, followed by today's count: Today is the 38th day of the Omer, which makes 5 weeks and 3 days of the Omer.

Thirty-ninth Blessing: Rejoicing in Accomplishment

Netzach sh'b'Yesod (Ney-tzach shah bah Yay-soad) is a lesson in appropriate pride. When you complete a task successfully, you can be justifiably proud without overstepping humility. Raising your spiritual level and taking happy stock in your progress is perfectly natural. A vibrant spiritual life feels good and clarifies your basic relationship with God and the people in your life. You've got every right to enjoy this. However, that doesn't make you better than anyone else— just happier!

Basically there's nothing wrong with stacking medals and prizes in a trophy case, as long as you understand that whatever good you accomplish gets done by the Grace of God. In that sense, *Netzach sh'b'Yesod* comes to mean that all glory should go to the Godhead, saying, "Thank, God, I made it."

Recite the standard blessing, followed by today's count: Today is the 39th day of the Omer, which makes 5 weeks and 4 days of the Omer.

Fortieth blessing: Artistry in Building

Hod sh'b'Yesod (Hoad shah bah Yay-soad) honors the artist in the builder. At a minimum, a building's foundation has to be solid and balanced. However, a Master Builder also makes the building shine forth in splendor, and he maintains his standard of beauty even on sections hidden from the user's view.

Spiritual development depends on a solid basis in Jewish law, tradition, and culture. Yet spiritual masters also can find beauty in their practice. As shown in the Talmudic story of Rabbi Yochanan and Resh Lakish [see the Thirtieth Blessing, above], Torah can be beautiful if you look for it, and if you already have an eye for beauty, you can maintain it even during serious discussions. *Hod sh'b'Yesod* says that, at its best, the foundation of spiritual practice shines forth both solid and splendid.

Recite the standard blessing, followed by today's count: Today is the 40th day of the Omer, which makes 5 weeks and 5 days of the Omer.

Forty-first blessing: Clinging to Mother Earth

Yesod sh'b'Yesod (Yay-soad shah bah Yay-soad) is the grounding Mother Earth provides for the lightning that descends from heaven. Like lightning hitting a target without a lightning conductor, our spiritual practice can burn us if it isn't well grounded.

The Kabbalah says that the Tree of Life has its roots in Paradise, alongside the famous Tree of Knowledge of Good and Evil. This suggests that no matter how spiritually developed you are, you shouldn't stop honoring Mother Earth. She bore your cradle, she furnishes your sustenance, and she holds your foundation. In return, you should preserve Mother Earth against neglectful pollution, mindless exploitation, and senseless waste. *Yesod sh'b'Yesod* says: Come down from the heights of spiritual splendor long enough to compost your kitchen waste.

Recite the standard blessing, followed by today's count: Today is the 41st day of the Omer, which makes 5 weeks and 6 days of the Omer.

Forty-second blessing: Single-minded Devotion

Malchut sh'b'Yesod (Mawl-choot shah bah Yay-soad) typifies total devotion to a cause. This quality resided quintessentially in our Biblical founding father, Joseph. He is a majestic figure, secure in his ability to steer himself through life. Perhaps even more than Abraham, Isaac, or Jacob, this late comer, Joseph, established the base of Jewish existence. If he hadn't established our base in Egypt, there would never have been an Exodus that led us to our Promised Land.

Therefore, it's not surprising that Joseph's story is the longest and most convoluted life history in the Five Books of Moses. Yet through all his vagaries, Joseph remained single-minded and steadfast, upholding the values he believed in.

The problem with Joseph, however, was that his single-mindedness was too extreme, as exemplified by how he followed up on the prophetic dream that Pharaoh had him interpret [Gen. 41]. Joseph correctly said the dream foretold seven good grain-producing years would be followed by seven miserable harvests. He wisely used his powers as Pharaoh's administrator to store grain from the good years to nourish the nation during the bad years. However, in the process, he monopolized the grain market and used the monopoly to make all of Egypt's ordinary citizens into slaves.

If Joseph's single-mindedness hadn't established the practice of slavery in Egypt, perhaps we Jews would not eventually have been enslaved in Egypt later on. Taking *Malchut sh'b'Yesod* to its extreme led to tragedy. Excess of any type produces misery, even if the underlying principle is indisputably valid.

Recite the standard blessing, followed by today's count: Today is the 42nd day of the Omer, which makes 6 entire weeks of the Omer.

The Sabbath of Yesod, Activity that Promotes Rest

At first blush, it would seem that a Sabbath within *Yesod* is an oxymoron. *Yesod,* after all, is at the vortex of human activity, especially creative activity. A second look at the issue, however, reveals that you have to have creative activity to have a Sabbath—or else, what would you be resting from? When God rested on the seventh day, he rested from ***creating.***

Jewish tradition mandates creative activity. The Masters say that you don't ***have to*** resume creative activities when the Sabbath ends after sundown on Saturday—you're just ***allowed to*** do so. However, they say you ***have to*** start creative work by Wednesday, so you work at least half a week, whether you're retired or not. Or else, the next Shabbat would be meaningless to you. That is the teaching of the Sabbath of Yesod.

SEVENTH WEEK: MALCHUT

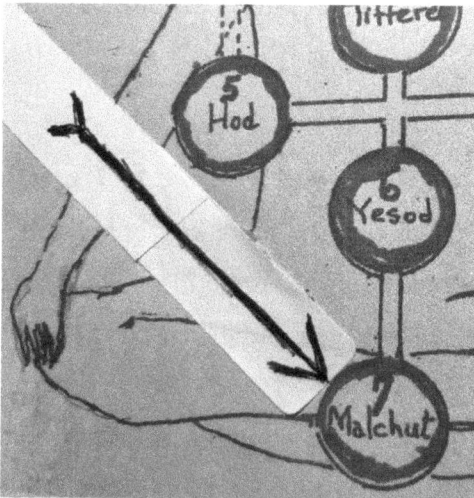

Malchut (Mawl-choot) "Kingdom, or Governance" comes as the "crowning moment" of the Omer period. It invites us to review the spiritual journey we started at Passover and to apply its lessons to usual daily existence.

Scripture points to a way to broaden our understanding. Immediately after the injunction to count the Omer and bring the appropriate sacrifices for *Shevuot,* the text advises: "And when you reap the harvest of your land, you shall not reap all the way to the edges of your field, or gather the gleanings of your harvest. You shall leave them for the poor and the stranger--so say I, the Lord Your God" [Lev. 23:22]. In other words, you don't just offer grain to honor God during a holiday—you also are responsible to other humans who may be in need of grain.

A Talmudic passage takes the train of thought leading from the Omer to the rule of King David. This train starts with The Book of Ruth, whose life was saved by benefiting from the injunction to leave part of any grain harvest for the stranger. Ruth arrives penniless in the Holy Land, and is able to feed herself and her mother-in-law by gleaning the grain fields of a distant kinsman named Boaz.

Her devotion to her mother-in-law and overall superb character bring her to the attention of Boaz, who eventually marries her despite the fact that Ruth is not particularly a "good catch." The whole clan of Boaz is rewarded for his generosity by having the exemplary King David be the great-grandson of Ruth and Boaz. And from the offspring from this same union, we are told, the Messiah will come.

King David personifies the *Sefirah* of *Malchut.* Jewish folklore pictures King David excelling in every field. Poetry? The best Psalms are Psalms of David. Music? The Harps of Heaven are fashioned by him. Military genius? He wins all battles. Devotion? He conceived the Temple. Savior? The true Messiah must be his descendant. Learning? The Wisdom of Great

Talmudic Learning comes from his mind. Even today, one of our most jubilant and popular folk songs goes *"David, Melech Yisrael, Chai ve-Kayam, "* David, the King of Israel, yet lives and will live forever."

Before David could attain his kingship, he first had to fearlessly confront and defeat evil, personified as the Philistine Goliath [I Samuel 17]. David of course defeats this 9 ½-foot giant, and if we, David's people, want to attain good governance over our lives, we must defeat our internal Goliath. We need to conquer the seemingly formidable negative impulses that are part of our nature. That's the ultimate message *of Malchut.*

Forty-third blessing: Grace in Governance

Chesed sh' b'Malchut (Chess-ed shah bah Mawl-choot) teaches us that the more kingly and the more developed we are, the more we need to remember grace and mercy. And the more we are in touch with the earthly rewards of our stewardship, the more we should remember our spiritual heritage.

Scripture makes this point in relating how King David arranged moving the Ark of the Covenant to Jerusalem [2 Samuel 6:13-15]. The Ark that the wandering Jews carried through the desert for 40 years had been put into storage after we came "home" and established the first State of Israel. Once David brings peace out of the turbulent conquest of the land, he becomes aware that the spiritual side of governance has been neglected.

Therefore, David orders the ark to be moved with great pomp and ceremony. *Chesed sh' b'Malchut* says that we should govern our lives the way that David governed Israel. We should periodically take stock of our turbulent life and reinvest it with its neglected spiritual side. **Recite the standard blessing**, followed by today's count: Today is the 43rd day of the Omer, which makes 6 weeks and 1 day of the Omer.

Forty-fourth blessing: Responsibility of Power

Gevurah sh' b'Malchut (Gev-voo-rah shah bah Mawl-choot) reminds us that royal strength needs to be matched with a deep sense of responsibility. Conversely, misjudgment can lead to tragic results—as illustrated by a story from King David's later life.

That story [II Samuel 15] starts when David's adult son Absalom decides to dethrone him. (Did the original story teller have his tongue in cheek when he called this rebellious son *Absalom* "Father of Peace"?)

Absalom succeeds in a palace revolution and King David has to flee with a contingent of loyal retainers to a sanctuary called Mahanayim across the river Jordan. Absalom, feeling threatened by his father's remaining power, decides to attack him at Mahanayim.

David stands at a highpoint in Mahanayim, watching his son's army approach, and he takes a critical look at *Gevurah sh 'b'Malchut*. Should he, by using his strength against his son, try to recapture his kingdom—and thereby lose the son whom he actually loved very much? Or should he surrender and lose his kingdom—but thereby spare his son?

David opts to defeat his son, who is killed in the process. David now can return to Jerusalem to resume his reign, but he is struck with great sadness.

Again he muses about whether he has done the right thing: "Oh, Absalom, my son!" he mourns, "would that I had died in your stead, Absalom, my son, my son."

This sad outcome shows that lack of responsibility can have dire consequences, especially in the case of absolute power. David's reign never regained its old glory, even though, in our hearts, King David has ever remained the Greatest of All Kings. In using strength and power at our disposal, we must assess whether we're using it appropriately to deal with the current challenge.

Recite the standard blessing, followed by today's count: Today is the 44th day of the Omer, which makes 6 weeks and 2 days of the Omer.

Forty-fifth blessing: Balance in Majesty

Tiferet sh 'b'Malchut (Tiff-air-et shah bah Mawl-choot) reminds us that, no matter how spiritually advanced we are, we can benefit from the insight of others if our life gets out of balance.

Again the life of King David comes to mind as an example. Scripture describes [II Samuel 11:14] that David had Uriah, one of his faithful guardsmen, killed so that, he, David, could acquire Uriah's wife, Bat-Sheva, for his royal harem. When the Prophet Nathan hears about this travesty, he comes to admonish David. The King takes the admonition in good grace and uses it to get himself back into balance.

The Prophet Nathan continued advising the King. He told David to put off building the Grand Temple, which was David's great dream; and he counseled him to name Solomon as his successor, bypassing Adonia, who was David's favorite. Perhaps David's most admirable trait is that he continued to keep Nathan on as his friend and adviser, no matter how bitter the advice.

Like the Ideal King, we should never be too proud or overly self-sufficient to listen to advice. Even if the message comes as a jolt, we need it to get ourselves back into balance.

Recite the standard blessing, followed by today's count: Today is the 45th day of the Omer, which makes 6 weeks and 3 days of the Omer.

Forty-sixth blessing: Victory With Majesty

Netzach sh'b'Malchut (Ney-tzach shah bah Mawl-choot) is a recurrent and difficult challenge. When the Great Leader wins a battle, how should he deal with the vanquished?

Early Jewish lore is unrelenting on this topic: No rights and no place for the defeated neighbors. For example, here are the military instructions God gives General Moses [Deut. 7]: "When the Lord your God brings you to the land that you are about to invade and occupy and He dislodges many nations before you—the Hittites, Girgashites, Amorites, Canaanites, Perizzites, Hivites, and Jebusites . . . and the Lord your God delivers them to you and you defeat them, you must doom them to destruction. Grant them no terms and give them no quarter ... Instead, this is what you shall do to them: You shall tear down their altars, smash their pillars, cut down their sacred posts, and consign their images to the fire."

Compare that to the generous policy of a modern-day Supreme Commander, General Yitzhak Rabin, who oversaw the Israeli armed forces during the Six-Day War of 1967. His armies beat the Egyptians so badly that they could have marched into Alexandria and torched the place. They could have done the same with Damascus after they had had beaten the Syrians. Yet the Israelis withdrew without damaging the defeated enemy; there was no action to " "tear down their altars, smash their pillars, cut down their sacred posts, and consign their images to the fire."

However, the aggressive actions of General Moses and the generous policy of General Rabin had the same results—never-ending animosity from the defeated neighbors. It will take an even wiser leader than Moses or Rabin to actualize the imperative of *Netzach sh'b'Malchut* and secure permanent peace for Israel.

Recite the standard blessing, followed by today's count: Today is the 46th day of the Omer, which makes 6 weeks and 4 days of the Omer.

Forty-seventh blessing: Splendor of Reign

Hod sh' b'Malchut (Hoad shah bah Mawl-choot) illuminates a serious modern quandary, namely how much splendor is too much? Supporting the grand monarchy of Great Britain costs British taxpayers untold millions per year, not to speak of lost revenues from tax breaks that the aristocracy enjoys. This has led to serious discussions of what service is being rendered by the splendor of royalty and whether taxpayers today can afford this luxury.

It doesn't take a major leap of thought to apply this question to our own lives, let's say a fancy wedding. Can a clear-eyed look at the cost justify such an event? We know that while a multi-course wedding dinner goes on in New York, poor folks in Eritrea can't even afford a cupcake and a candle to celebrate a wedding. Instead of money going to *Hod* (splendor), should it go to *Chesed* (charity)?

Defenders of costly weddings and parties say that the money spent isn't just thrown out—it helps sustain our economy. Look at the benefits that are generated just by the flowers for the wedding—let's say just the gardenias. They provide work for the gardener who grows them, the delivery service that transports them, the decorators who place them in the wedding hall, and probably several others.

We could divert this money to staving off hunger in Eritrea. If we did, however, we would deprive the wedding providers back in the United States from their source of income.

Furthermore, the argument goes, all *of Hod* isn't ostentation. A well-planned wedding and party sustains religion, invests wedding vows with communal support, lifts up the spirits of those attending, and gives them a chance to shmooze, dance, dine, and feel happy. Can we put a monetary limit on generating happiness?

Several of my friends have chosen a middle ground. They designate part of the budget for their wedding for charity. What's left still gives plenty of people work and plenty of celebrants a good time. How do you make the cut between charity and celebration? That's the question posed by *Hod sh' b'Malchut.*

Recite the standard blessing, followed by today's count: Today is the 47th day of the Omer, which makes 6 weeks and 5 days of the Omer.

Forty-eighth blessing. Foundation of Majesty

Yesod sh' b'Malchut (Yay-soad shah bah Mawl-choot) asks, *What background and experience do you need to be a king?* In theory, this is a valid question. In practice, most king candidates don't have to present any qualifications. If they succeed earlier kings in their genealogy, they just have to be born in the right place at the right time. If they seize power on their own, they're just Lord of the Jungle.

Kings themselves like to say that they get their authority by divine appointment. They like to picture a Divine chain of command with God at the top, and the king one rung below him as managing director, who in turn appoints middle and low-ranking managers called nobles and knights. I don't subscribe to this justification of royalty, which seems just plain self-serving. It leads to the next question, *By what authority does God get to be in charge of everything?*

To me, the whole issue of divine appointment is wrong. I believe the issue is not one of royal authority but one of creativity. God created for six representational days, and God keeps creating and he urges and inspires us humans to create alongside him.

Recite the standard blessing, followed by today's count: Today is the 48th day of the Omer, which makes 6 weeks and 6 days of the Omer.

Forty-ninth blessing: The blessing of completion

Malchut sh' b'Malchut (Mawl-choot shah bah Mawl-choot) seems to ask, *Now that we've completed our count, what about the future?*

The Omer count walks you up a golden staircase toward a hopeful future. Jewish lore consistently visualizes that hopeful view as a bountiful harvest gathered from the fields and vineyards of our own land. The Prophet Amos says it so clearly [Amos 9:14-15]: "I will bring back my exiled people Israel; they will rebuild the ruined cities and live in them. They will plant vineyards and drink their wine; they will make gardens and eat their fruit. I will plant Israel in their own land, never again to be uprooted from the land I have given them," says the Lord your God.

Reaching Shavuot by counting the Omer presupposes that we'll keep on growing spiritually, convinced that life makes sense, that our existence has a purpose, and that we can rise up spirituality to a higher level. Together, we have discovered a blessing in each of 49 days, good practice for finding goodness in every future day to come.

Recite the standard blessing, followed by today's count: Today is the 49th day of the Omer, which makes seven complete weeks of the Omer.

The Sabbath of Malchut, a King's Respite

Can a busy king ever rest? We don't have a king in Jerusalem today, but we did have a prime minister who had to decide what to do when enemies attacked on the Day of Yom Kippur. When do you spring into action on a day of rest—what justifies the decision to break the rest? What defines a true emergency? Again, I see this as a matter of balance, so clearly expressed in the pairs of Sefirot that stand side by side in the Tree of Life. We saw that in the balance of *Chesed* and *Gevurah*, between generosity and a power grab.

Sabbath observance is healing and a lift up from the humdrum of the week to a spiritual high. It is not an iron rule that can't be broken—a mistaken notion dramatically expressed by one of my neighbors in the Orthodox community in Baltimore. A few years ago, I heard him in the street one Shabbat, yelling for help. *What did he need?*

It turned out that there was an electrical fire in his house, and he needed someone to turnoff his master switch to stop feeding the fire! Shabbat concerns made him unwilling to pull the switch himself, even in so acting, he fed his panic—hardly a restful Sabbath activity. On the other hand, many people I know set their Sabbath limits much too low. And the limits get pushed down week by week because of stuff that "absolutely must be done."

The Sabbath of *Malchut* teaches us to avoid both extremes. Setting our personal Sabbath limits is a serious responsibility, and the last Sabbath of the Omer is a good time to reassess where you want to take your stand.

ARRIVING AT SHAVUOT

by Dr. Ismar Schorsch, Chancellor,
Jewish Theological Seminary, NY, NY.
Abridged and used with permission

Shavuot and Passover are linked by the daily counting of the Omer, so that the two holidays are inextricably related. However, *Shavuot* is with us for only a brief two days, and it never enjoyed the popularity of *Pesach,* that glorious, week-long holiday with its elaborate ritual drama and stirring universal message. Still, *Shavuot* should not suffer from inattention because, since the two holidays are linked, *Pesach* otherwise loses the closure it needs.

So let us take a deeper look at *Shavuot.* I think it addresses the basic question of what we are to do with our freedom. Without Sinai, the exodus from Egypt yields little more than a formless state of national disorder. With Sinai, the Exodus story takes on the brilliance of a Constitution that protects individual liberty.

Shavuot may repel some of us because we have lost our faith in amanuensis, the literal revelation that diligently records every word dictated from on high. But already the ancient rabbis dared to restrict this concept somewhat.

For example: There are two sets of blessings and curses in the Torah. The first last week, in Chapter 26 of Leviticus, is always recited in the synagogue just prior to Shavuot. The second set, near the end of Deuteronomy in Chapter 28, is always recited prior to Rosh Hashanah.

The second set contains a particularly long and grim list of imprecations, so harrowing that the Torah reader is obligated to lower his or her voice when reciting them. In interpreting this heavy-handed damnation, the rabbis focused on the difference in length and venom between the two sets. In Leviticus, God offers 22 blessings against 8 curses. In Deuteronomy, there are only 8 blessings but 22 curses, the exact reverse.

The rabbis concluded from this comparison that that only the first set of curses in Leviticus was the word of God. The second set in Deuteronomy, they decided, came entirely from Moses. They said this indicates a contrast between divine and human anger. God is seen as the more compassionate of the two.

With this sensitive *Midrash* (Mid-rawsh) "interpretation of Scripture," the Rabbis made Torah more human. The issue, they seem to say, is not who wrote the Torah, but what we do with it.

In dealing with another Bible verse the rabbis found unpalatable [Ezek. 20:25], they suggested that it refers to a situation in which "a person reads the Torah without music, or studies Scripture without melody." The charge of this *Midrash* to us is to put Judaism to music, to make it a work of art. It sets us a model: Not to carp over the likelihood of revelation, but to imbue and enlarge Torah with human artistry and ingenuity.

Judaism has always conceived humanity as God's partner. And partnership is the note which ends the magnificent prophetic passage [Hosea 2:21-22] read on the Shabbat preceding Shavuot. In it, God renews the covenant by retaking Israel as His bride:

> And I will espouse you forever. I will espouse you with righteousness
> and justice, and with goodness and mercy. And I will espouse you
> with faithfulness. Then shall you be devoted to the Lord.

This partnership is the challenge of *Shavuot.*